WITHDRAWN

HOW-TO SPORTS

BASEBALL

Paul Joseph
ABDO & Daughters

Published by Abdo & Daughters, 4940 Viking Drive, Suite 622, Edina, Minnesota 55435.

Printed in the United States.

Cover Photo credits: Superstock
Interior Photo credits: Superstock
Allsport photo, page 23, 25

Edited by Bob Italia

Library of Congress Cataloging-in-Publication Data

Joseph, Paul, 1970-
    Baseball / Paul Joseph
        p. cm. -- (How-To-Sports)
    Includes index.
    Summary: Explains how to play baseball, with a discussion of the equipment, rules, pitching and catching, and the strategy involved in offense and defense.
     ISBN 1-56239-644-7
    1. Baseball--Juvenile literature. [1. Baseball.] I. Title. II. Series:
    GV867.5.J68 1996   96-6412
    796.357--dc20   CIP
                                                                                            AC

Contents

How the Game Began

Baseball is called the national game of the United States. It is also popular in Japan, the Caribbean, and Latin America.

In 1839, Abner Doubleday invented the game of baseball in Cooperstown, New York. He made up a set of rules and guidelines that are still used today.

The first pro team began playing in 1869. They were called the Cincinnati Red Stockings. Because of Cincinnati's popularity, many more professional baseball teams formed across the country.

Today, thousands of people play this great sport. There are many different leagues in which to play, including **T-ball**, **Little League**, high school, and college leagues. If an athlete becomes good, there is also **Major League Baseball.**

Before playing baseball, become familiar with the **equipment**, rules, positions, and how to play as a team. Then you will see why baseball is so much fun!

Baseball is considered America's national pastime.

The Equipment

The proper **equipment** is needed to play baseball. This includes a bat, helmet, glove, and protective gear for the **catcher**.

Baseball equipment.

A player can use an aluminum or wooden bat. Choose one that is easy to grip and swing. Then you can hit the ball more often and farther.

A player must always wear a helmet when batting and running the **bases**. The helmet should fit snugly so it doesn't fall off.

Choose a glove that fits your hand. A loose glove makes it hard to catch the ball.

The **catcher** and **first base player** have different gloves. The first base player has a glove shaped like a half-moon. This shape helps the player scoop up balls thrown into the dirt.

The catcher's glove is round, which gives the **pitcher** a large target. It also has plenty of padding to protect the catcher's hand.

The catcher also must wear special **equipment** for protection against wild pitches and **foul balls**. This equipment includes a facemask with a throat guard, a chest protector, and shin guards to protect the legs.

facemask

throat guard

chest protector

glove

shin guard

Learning the Basics of Baseball

Once a player learns to **grip**, throw, and catch the ball, he or she will have a skill that is shared with **Major League** players. These basic skills never change, so they can be used for a lifetime.

The basics begin with the baseball, which often weighs 5.5 ounces (.15 kg.). Grip the ball the same way every time you throw. First, put your pointer and middle fingers across the wide **seams**. Hold the ball with the inside edge of your thumb on the opposite side. Your ring finger and pinkie should rest on the side of the ball. Keep your hand relaxed.

Opposite page:
A baseball weighs
5.5 ounces (.15 kg).

Your legs should be shoulder-width apart. Keep your eyes on the target. Then stride toward the target by pushing off your back foot. At the same time, bring your arm and hand over your shoulder. Release the ball with a strong wrist snap.

When catching the ball, a player should stand in a comfortable, relaxed position. Bend your knees and spread your feet about shoulder-width apart. Be ready for the ball at all times.

Glove position for catching the ball below the waist (left) and above the waist (right).

If the ball is thrown below your waist, catch the ball with your glove fingers pointed down. If it's above your waist, the glove fingers should be pointed up.

The Offense

The main goal on **offense** is to **hit** the baseball. Once the ball is hit, the player must run the **bases**.

Before it is your turn to hit, pick a bat that can be swung easily. The bat should feel light. The handle should fit comfortably in your hands.

Step up to home plate and position yourself inside the **batter's box**. Make sure you **grip** the bat properly. If you are a right-handed batter, put your right hand above your left hand. Left-handers place their left hand above the right. Hold the bat firmly, but not too tight. You will hit better if you are relaxed.

Your **stance** should be relaxed and loose. Legs should be shoulder-length apart. Hold the bat at shoulder height and keep it upright.

The proper batting stance before hitting the baseball.

To swing the bat, shift your weight to your back foot, keeping your eye on the ball. Then move your front foot forward and take a level swing while extending your arms and keeping your head still. Your weight should shift to your front foot.

After you hit the ball in **fair territory**, you must run the **bases**. Good base running is important. You don't need to be fast to run the bases well. But you must know where the ball is on the field.

Arm extension is important when hitting the baseball.

After hitting the ball, run along the **foul line** toward first base. You must reach first base before the **defensive** team can throw the ball to their **first base player**. If the ball is hit far enough, continue running for second base.

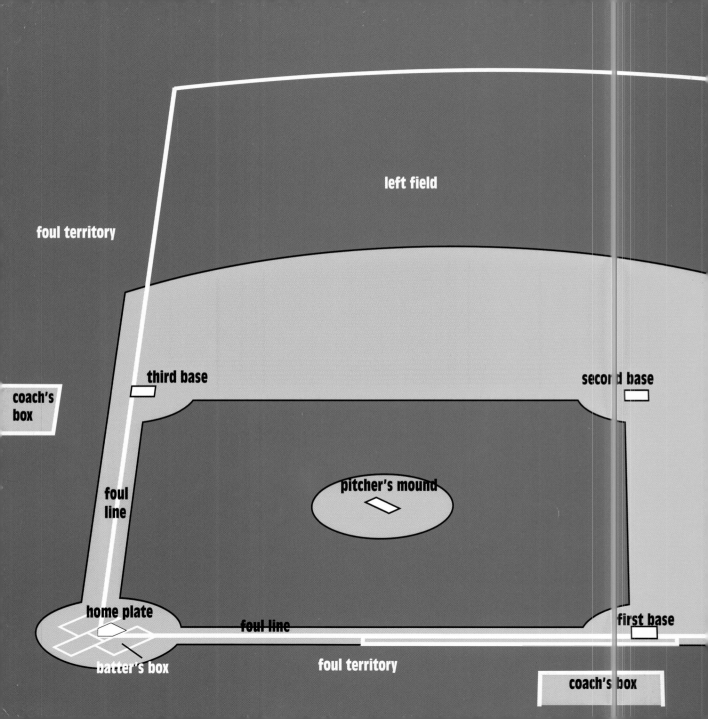

left field

foul territory

coach's box

third base

second base

foul line

pitcher's mound

home plate

first base

batter's box

foul line

foul territory

coach's box

How-To
Baseball

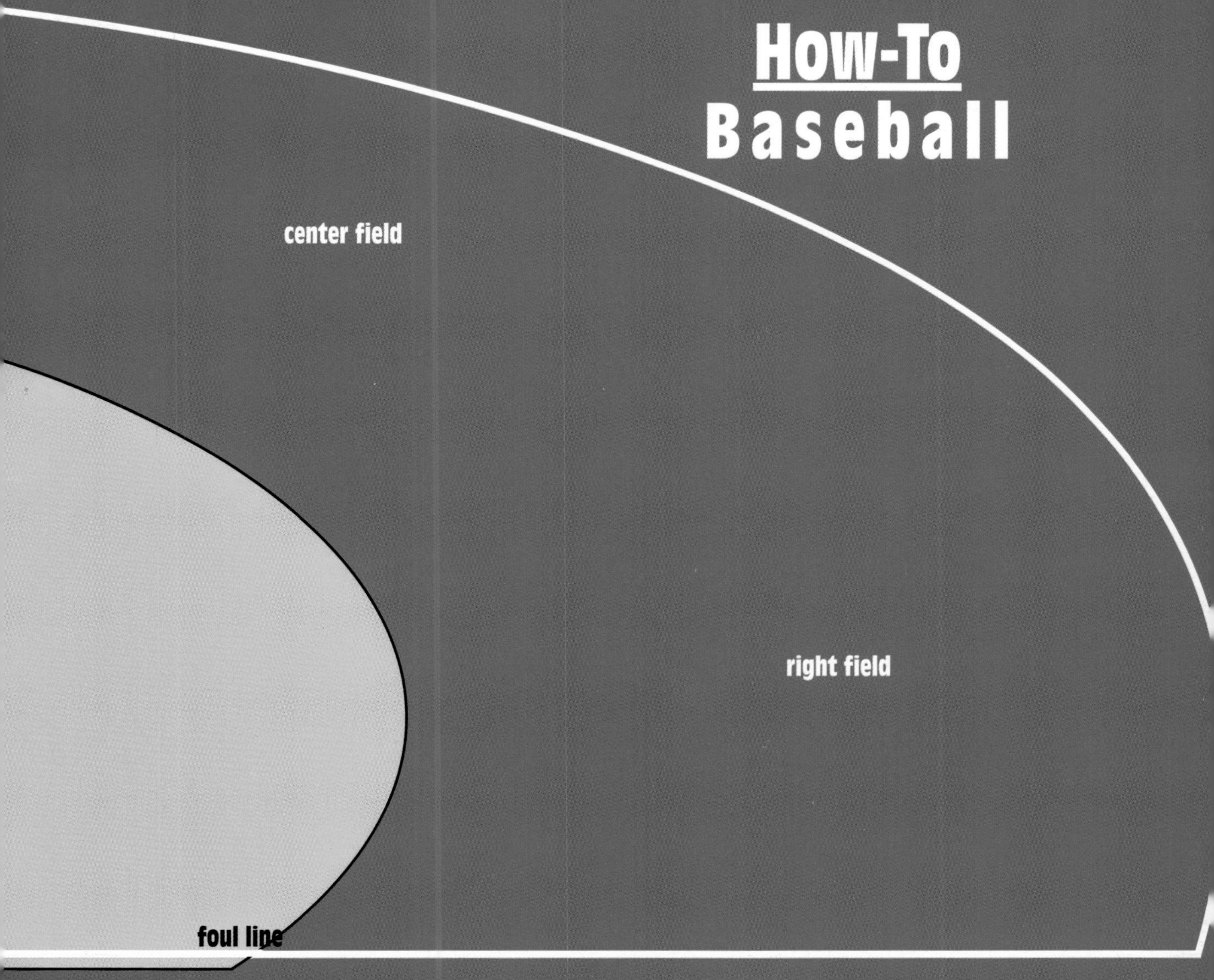

center field

right field

foul line

foul territory

The Defense

In baseball, the **defense** has many positions. There are **infielders**, **outfielders**, a **pitcher**, and a **catcher**. The infielders are the first line of a team's defense. More balls are hit to infielders than

Fielders must be ready at all times in case a ball is hit their way.

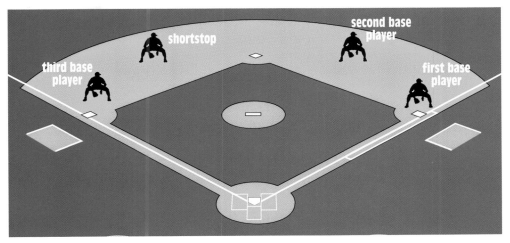

The infield positions.

outfielders. **Infielders** must be ready at all times. Because baseballs are hit fast to them, infielders also have to make quick decisions.

The infield has four positions: the **first base player**, **second base player**, **third base player**, and **shortstop**. When playing an infield position, keep your legs shoulder-length apart and your weight forward. Bend your knees, and keep your hands in front of your body. Stay relaxed so you can move quickly forward, backward, left, or right.

First base players must watch for ground balls. They must also cover the base to get the runner out when the ball is thrown to them.

Second base players play between first and second base. Many baseballs are hit to them. They must also cover second base.

Most balls are hit to **shortstops**. They must be very quick and have a strong arm to throw the ball to first base. Shortstops have the most territory of any **infielder**. They stand between second and third base and must help cover them.

Third base players play the "hot corner." The hardest-hit balls come their way. Because most batters are right handed, it is natural for them to hit the ball toward the third base player. These players must also have a strong throwing arm because they have the longest throw to first base.

From left: the batter, pitcher, catcher, and umpire.

19

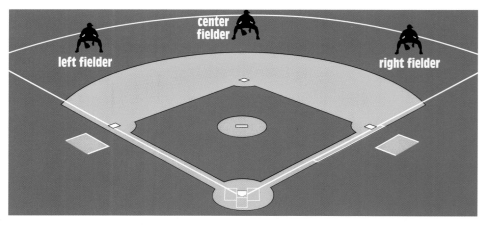

The outfield positions.

The **outfield** has three positions: the **left fielder**, **center fielder**, and **right fielder**. These players must be fast and cover a lot of ground. They must also have strong arms to throw the ball a long way.

Center fielders cover the most ground so they should be the fastest runners. The right fielders should have the strongest arms because they sometimes have to throw to third base. **Left fielders** should be the best fielders because most baseballs are hit to them.

All **outfielders** should have a good **stance**—relaxed, and ready as soon as the **pitcher** throws the ball.

An outfielder's main job is to catch fly balls. When one is hit to you, keep your eyes on the ball. Station yourself under the ball and hold your glove up and open, ready to catch the ball.

All **defensive** positions are important, each working toward one goal—to keep the opposing team from scoring!

Pitching and Catching

The **pitcher** and **catcher** make up the **battery**. They have the most difficult jobs on **defense**. Pitchers must not only throw the ball, they must play the **infield**. Many balls are hit at them, and they must be quick with their glove.

But pitching is their number one job. Pitchers must always concentrate on throwing a good pitch. Beginners should practice their **delivery** and learn to throw **strikes**.

Before throwing the baseball, stretch your arm and get it warmed up. Use your entire body when you pitch, not just your arm. This will help prevent injuries.

Opposite page:
The pitcher delivers a
pitch toward home plate.

A **catcher** must have proper **equipment**. The catching position is a difficult job because this player must catch many pitches. The catcher must also have a strong arm to throw to second base when a **base runner** tries to **steal**.

The catcher takes a lot of pounding from foul tips, pitches in the dirt, and runners trying to score. But the position also is fun and rewarding. Catchers often are the team leader, and get the most action.

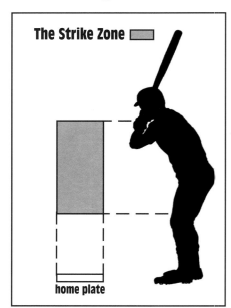

The strike zone is directly above home plate and between the batter's knees and shoulders. Any pitch thrown outside the strike zone is called a ball.

Playing the Game

When learning to play baseball, a player should try all the positions. This way, you will know which one you like and play best. When you begin playing in a league, your **coach** will place you in a position that you play well. You will probably play there most of the time.

A baseball team has different positions.

In a baseball game, there are two teams: one bats and the other puts nine players in the field. A batter will **strike out**, get a **hit**, or **walk**. A strike out is three strikes. A walk is four balls.

There are nine **innings** in a game, and three outs to each inning. An out is made when a batter strikes out, hits the ball to a fielder who catches it before the ball hits the ground, or is thrown out while running the **bases**.

If the batter reaches a base safely, another batter tries to advance or score the **base runner**. To score a run, the base runner must reach home plate safely.

When three outs are made, the fielding team goes up to bat while the batting team takes the field. This occurs nine times before the game is over. The team with the most runs wins.

Opposite page:
Baseball is a team sport.

Fair Play and Team Spirit

Baseball is a team game. Always cheer and encourage your teammates when they make a good play. Also remember to support them when they make a mistake.

Baseball can be a difficult game, especially when you are learning to play. Practice the basics, learn many positions, and be a team player. Always be a good sport whether you win or lose.

If you work hard and have a good attitude, baseball can be rewarding and fun.

Glossary

base runner - an offensive player who runs from base to base.

bases - places on the field that the base runner runs to after hitting the ball. There are three bases: first, second, and third base.

batter's box - the area on either side of home plate in which batters must position themselves to hit.

battery - the pitcher and catcher of a baseball team.

catcher - the player behind home plate who catches pitches and throws out base runners.

center fielder - the outfielder positioned between the right and left fielder.

coach - the person who is in charge of the team and makes all of the decisions involving the team and the game.

defense - the side that has players in the infield and outfield and tries to get the offense out.

delivery - the motion a pitcher develops to throw the ball to home plate.

equipment - things you need to play baseball, such as a bat, ball, helmet, and glove.

fair ball - a ball hit into fair territory.

fair territory - the part of the baseball field between the foul lines.

first base player - the infielder who covers first base.

foul ball - a ball hit into foul territory.

foul lines - the straight, white lines that extend in fair territory from home plate, past third and first base, and along the edge of left and right field. The foul lines separate fair territory from foul territory.

foul territory - the part of the baseball field outside the foul lines.

grip - to take hold of an object.

hitting - to swing the bat and strike the ball into fair territory after the pitch is thrown.

infield - the part of the field where the pitcher, first, second, and third base players, the shortstop, and all the bases are located.

inning - a division of a baseball game during which each team has a turn at bat.

left fielder - the player on the left side of the outfield.

Little League - a baseball league played by children ranging from the age of 9 to 12.

Major League Baseball - a league of highest classification in professional baseball. It has the best players in the world and consists of 28 teams from different cities in the United States and Canada.

offense - the side that is up to bat and is trying to score runs against the defense.

outfield - the area of a baseball field just beyond the infield that has the left, right, and center fields.

pitcher - the player who pitches the ball to the batter.

right fielder - the outfielder who covers all balls hit to the right side of the outfield.

seams - the line formed by sewing together two pieces of leather that form the baseball.

second base player - the position where the player stands between first and second base and fields balls and covers second base.

shortstop - the position where the player is between the second and third base player. They are responsible for covering the most ground and helping with second and third.

stance - a way of standing; the position taken by an athlete while playing.

steal - when a base runner advances a base while a pitch is thrown.

strike - a pitch swung at and missed or fouled away; also, a pitch that passes through the strike zone but not swung at.

strike out - To put out or be put out on three strikes.

T-Ball - a game played by young children that uses the same rules as baseball except players hit from a tee instead of being pitched to.

third base player - the position where the player plays close to third base and is responsible for fielding and covering the base.

walk - to advance to first base after the pitcher throws four balls.

Index